More Praise for Sally Albiso Award Winner
In the Salt by Caitlin Dwyer

I was astonished by the daring and virtuosity of this collection. *In the Salt* is part love song to a child, part homage to Homer's Penelope. If "Motherhood is a kind of wildness, a loosening," we find in these poems a painful, tentative hope, the world pulled to tatters by crisis, each morning the threads taken up again.

—Bethany Reid, author of
2023 Sally Albiso Award Winner
The Pear Tree: elegy for a farm
& 2025 Sally Albiso Award Judge

IN THE SALT

IN THE SALT

Caitlin Dwyer

MoonPath Press

Poetry
ISBN 978-1-970256-00-0

Cover art: *You Were Once a Part of Me* by Brenan Dwyer

Author photo by Lyle Poulin

Wave icon by Paul from thenounproject.com

Book design by Tonya Namura using
Minion Pro (text) and Good Pro (display)

MoonPath Press is dedicated to publishing the finest poets
living in the U.S. Pacific Northwest.

MoonPath Press
PO Box 2220
Newport, OR 97365-0163

MoonPathPress@gmail.com

https://MoonPathPress.com

For Quinn

Of bodies chang'd to various forms, I sing:
—Ovid

I reintroduced myself to myself, this time
a mother. After which, nothing was ever the same.
—Camille Dungy

Contents

IN THE SALT

Song to My Child in the Salt

You in the starless
darkness, stay still.

We don't want you knowing
too much already, when the answers

are scraped inside your bone-
wood, like the tracks of sea snails

over soft corals, grooves in water
left by a departing shark.

You in the raft of my body,
you in my secret current,

let me count for you
the songs of becoming:

first the soundless whisper of jellies
gently flexing their satin bodies.

Second the swarms of prey-fish
that make their purpose known

in the gathering of many bodies
into a single clump of flesh.

Deep in the salt, instinct
is a kind of wisdom.

Your clasped fists.
Your wet, dark ears.

When your eyes open, the salt
will be plucked from your skin

and placed in the sky,
a dull, gray glitter,

tracery of light like
the sleepless song of whales,

whose rumbles draw
long silver lines of migration

cold current to cold current,
dot to shimmering dot.

Penelope Pregnant

He's going to leave me. With every kick
the ground drops out, as when an airplane
lurches, suddenly loses altitude.
Two feet, or twenty. I grip the seat.
Next to me the bearded man is singing.
He craves this feeling, its weightlessness,
the body briefly lifted from its shell
and hanging above itself like a skinned shade.
I clutch my aching wrists. I solve the crossword
in ink and tuck it into the seat. Later,
I will walk until the kicking soothes, wander
among fog-shapes, skitter of snakes and
morning birds, and feel the thin air burn.

When we first married, he used to walk with me.
Where are we going? he would ask. The ruins
of the temple, the ridge with its vistas
of curling shore and wavery, metallic sea.
We're just walking, I replied, and now
he does not come. There is no place to jump
into the waves and feel the brief glory
of weightlessness. There is only my belly
like a carbuncle beneath sore fingers, knuckles
numb from picking out knots, and the stitch
of my breath, which grows tauter every day.
I cannot climb as high as I once did.
I cannot any more cast ripples in the wells
with my mere reflection, cause a riot
with my undone hair. The child
has come between us. Which is to say,
my body has. When the plane lurches
I grab his hand, and he grins. *Wasn't that fun?*
But I have already fallen out of my old self,
am wandering shadowless among the hills,

my son a bright spot in my belly,
and the swollen moon falling out, out,
tugging me up with it into an unfamiliar sky.

Ultrasound

searchlight strobes dark waves
broad-beams catch on curtain edges
on the stacked white vertebrae of
lantern fish, flashlight fish
beasts of the bathypelagic
silver-bodied ghosts with
pale blank moons across
pupils, milk-foam mouths

sifting water through the sieve
of fingerbones is not
a substitute for an oar
the currents are so strong and
the fish with their spiny nubs
of lips are gumming the raft
toward the Argand lamp
with its stench of whale oil
its smokeless flame

heat singes the scales
of sea creatures, crumbling
their firm muscle into ash
soot along the edges of silver plates
dark lacquer of tintype
emulsion of brine

in the aphotic nothing
develops they say but
the dead who are unchanging
ever present and white
in the cores of their eyes

but then you no longer
belong to them

Odysseus at the Solar Eclipse

The wires of our world are thin
but tensile, tugging at the great bodies.
They resist, and then they give.
Sometimes it feels best not to fight the urge
to disappear, so that only flickers
escape in a corona, survive the elision.
The detail work can be very beautiful,
like those machines at the zoo
full of thin chains and hand cranks
which wipe away your penny's face,
replace it with some rare, stamped scene.
My father calls this shyness but it is
I think a curiosity to see other things shine,
more than a desired darkness of my own.
As a child's best view of a show is not
front row but wings, among the ropes
and luminaires, the quick-change tutus.
That is, the gearshifts themselves
were always the real attraction, the penny
a pleasant afterthought. As a child
I wanted to see the grinding.

Sometimes now that feeling lingers,
like a wishing wisp caught in a cobweb,
all the wish gone out of it. My father
says that this is mechanistic, to think
only of the whirring and clinking,
each dropped prop and discarded skirt.
Only gears still shifting with the yes yes yes
of each crank, a reduction of awe.
Anyone could remake the world
if they just watched hard enough.
Anyone could observe cycle upon cycle
and begin to etch the outline of the sun

into the back of their retinas: a burned-
on souvenir, blindness in the shape
of a map of the world's turning.
Don't you want mystery? he asked me
as we stood under the darkening morning
sky, watching moon-shapes impress
themselves on the grass. Don't you want
some things to remain unknowable?
I said yes to appease him but I want
to know everything. I want to watch
a fitted tooth catching another and turning
hard until the thing we call miracle
is neither trick nor mere result but something
in between—predicable and still wondrous, visible only
when the great barrenness is overwritten,
and we come upon a small and unexpected
embossed scene: firm ridges of antlers,
a place pressed smooth for a copse of birch,
the rippling gelatin silver of a pond in which,
who knows, there could be cutthroat trout.

Waste Thread

Silver-tipped rhododendrons.
Lichen-speckled bark.
I close my eyes and dream of rain, wake
and dream of rain. My eyes blur
when I try to focus. When I gaze out
of my eyes and not my head, I feel alive.
Nose in the wet soil. Songs of worm-trace
and limestone, shell-break, calcium pulver.
Phlox in the cracks. I close my eyes
and sugar-syrup coats my tongue, crystallized
honey cracked against a bad tooth.

Penelope's Nightmares

Fishhooks pierced the pupils
and the colors bled

like loose roe into the streams
Wet flesh and

unblinking gaze
They told me everything

Their eyes had been plucked from them
like mussels from the shell

Ten thousand red eyes
sank to the bottom

My husband's boat passed above them
full of men eating fish

He held a dagger in the shape of
a woman's body

I wanted to scream but
mouth, black and fuzzy

Woke clutching the skin between my eyebrows
I captured it in fog—fingers cool

on the glass, anemones blooming
from his dead hands

An eye in the center of my head
Great and unblinking I stumbled
over it in dreams and it stuck
Affixed like a burr
to the hem of a dress only
much itchier

I clawed at it tried
to pop it like a zit it
bulged but
did not burst—I woke

with red marks on my
forehead and
the story on my palms

Through bug eyes, faceted and iridescent
the world tumbles in its hexagons
Every facet contains a different story
I trip over furniture trying to see

out my window: pines, waves
desert mineral waver and blend
A hundred seascapes, all equally possible
I wake up screaming, my shins

rubbed raw and pink, throat hoarse
My breath frictions out of me
like wind clatters stiff wash
wet weight fighting the squall

I clip sheets to the lines but
grow dizzy with the flapping
Like insects, the dreams rise up
off their impalings and reassert themselves

Waste Threads

Motherhood is a kind of wildness, a loosening
of edges, tearing up of grommets once securely pegged.

Things flap like frantic hands. But also
deep wells. Dark pools that had lain hidden under tarps.

ECMO

It's hope, that dreadful, soothing offer, I cannot take.
So far, I'm still a mother, but the word is hospital gown,
    thin sheath.
I shiver. In the company of drip and beep, we wait.

Our child, a creature torn from us, intubated
and cannulated, blood looping out in ruby wreaths.
It's that color, that gorgeous red, I cannot take.

Half-zombied, propped with pillows, he can't inflate
his lungs. Machines outsource his breathing, while
in the company of drip and beep, we wait.

Can you pack the lungs' crannies? Can you automate a
    heartbeat?
Yes, these days, the body can give up beating, be deceived
to abdicate its pulse. His blood in two thick streams is
    taken,

a flow they must keep clear of clots until his shock abates
and eyes—what color are they?—finally peek.
Amid the drone of drips and beeps, we wait, but

I can see the fluttering. Under the eyelids, the tubes, the
    sedation,
he's dreaming. There's a body laid out, but a boy beneath.
It's the fear, that unbearable clot, I cannot take.
In its company, singing softly to drown the beeps, we wait.

Fentanyl

I asked three times. Say I was scared.
Say I just wanted to be left alone.
Say I was, and it hurt. Was I spared?
He wasn't. The nurses said he wasn't going home.

Say I just wanted to be left alone,
knowing hurt would hit hard when the meds wore off.
The nurses said he wasn't going home,
would be transferred ward to ward, taken from me,

so knowing hurt would hit hard when the meds wore off,
I asked for more. Something for the pain. Not his body,
transferred ward to ward, taken from me.
Not his name, which I didn't know. Fentanyl,

I asked. Give me something for the pain. Not his body.
I asked three times. Say I was scared.
Say I didn't know his name, didn't want to, just in case
he wasn't spared. Say I was, and it hurt.

Heparin

"Heparin to 36," the nurse requests,
but the ruby sheen that is your blood
clamped off looks no thinner.
No milky flush, just the swish of cells

out and away, silk-red, a sexy hue
if it weren't your body on bypass, your baby
blood entombed in hard plastic and swept fast
through narrow, artificial veins. To keep

from clotting, they say, the drug will dissolve
any lurch in the machinery, drag waste away
and cleanse the circuit. It doesn't solve anything
to think of rivers, but I do—how in March

the snowmelt snaps down the saplings, digs
at the sand under boulders until they lift away
and crash downstream, only to stall
in shallow pools, dam the creamy

churn. I think of salmon habitat, and trout;
shady, log-jammed deeps. With practiced ease
the nurse asks for another increase,
silvers the flow. A rehearsal for the way

an animal spirit breaks from its body, thinning
as it slips from skin, slides beneath,
gradually guttering away. Your blood,
skim and flushing. But in the brain, we hope,

banks are not yet breached, the vessels holding.
Better bleed than clot? Either way the lines
blot. Don't move your fingers
until the ink dries. Don't move at all;

you'll ruin the polish.
Anticoagulant worries into the pulse.
Mechanical thaw, sheen of oil:
convulse, shimmer in the bad water.

Chest Tube

Pull in. Push. Your breathing stutters.
We try suction, try oscillating your thorax,
the core of you lifted and fluttered like
a bumblebee's wing. Air cracks

upward, a deep-sea diver's burps: little bloats,
the way we process bad news, dissolving it one
drop at a time. Jitters floating upward through
the blood until they burst, become solvent,

but the body is no solution: "The chest cavity
will inflate if we remove the tube." Grief
feels like a cave, ribs bracketing dark reefs,
deep, crude fissures from which vapor steams,

seeps, sticks. "A toxic atmosphere"
is how my father-in-law describes the ward.
"But the nurses are terrific." I breathe
the antiseptic pallor, the clean, guarded,

empty scent. "He has to heal that hole,"
they explain, as if what mattered was will.
As if splayed and intubated the body could control
its own fiasco, fire through billions

of neurons, ignite each deliberately. Choose:
close. No more punctures just above the ribs
where the lungs creak, the loose flaps of the body
hissing as they pass air, hissing as they resist

the illusion of wholeness. Flex and thrust.
Pull hard. A gurgling as the vapors rise
through water (just the tissue, just
damp cloth, vise grip, wrung out

and hung to dry). Air in the empty pockets,
packed around the heart like cushioning papers
around Christmas pears. Despair pulls
hard, insistent tug. Don't crack. But surface,

soon, or face the bends. Swirl creamer
in hospital coffee, imagine the way the ocean
inflates with the tide. The way it rends the shore,
tattered hollow wood, then rises to cover the damage.

Between

Winter night. High cold haze
and the stars prickly
burrs of light. I was content

to let other people map your
body onto the world; there was
still a faint tracery on my bones,

snail-etchings that glistened
with the leaving of the animal.
I didn't know you were dying.

Or I knew, but I didn't want to.
I gave myself ten more minutes
before I knew. Ten more hours.

Two days. Three days. Ten days
before I held you and by then
I understood what the word

decouple means, as in the winch
has decoupled from the tractor,
as in the stars have decoupled from

their antagonistic marriage, as in
the body no longer holds in itself
a constellation of otherness.

Instead, the body understands
it has slipped out of its
beckonings. It wears unkempt

night worry. It wears unraveling.
What I did not do that night
will always be between us.

Waste Thread

No one told the woman she was a fool but it became clear
over time that she could not hold her shape without a
    new container.

Penelope Fears Sleep

I took my needle to the stitches
my knife to the bed-
sheets, cutting open feather
duvets, spilling hollow bird-
edges everywhere

I pressed them to my face
felt them stick in
my ears, up my nose
The weft was full of rachis
Barbs clinging

I ate quills, worried, then realized
all the points were snipped
There was no scarring
and the story wrote itself
in my throat
A gentle scratch

I see her in thirty facets
move swiftly over the beach
toward him

She sometimes appears as
a mountain lion, sometimes
a seal

Now she nuzzles his arm
with her great lioness face
Wedge-shaped, heavy
jaw, her pink nose drawing
wet shapes on his skin

I saw her I saw
the way her great paws
laid on protection
The way his hands lay
over her body like
a spell

Every night it changes
Sometimes she is a hawk
and she bites his ears
until he kneels
Sometimes she flops
on the beach, yelping
for her pups, and when
he kneels next to her
she folds him in her wet
rubbery skin and he
disappears

She is not a lion
but a netting

A lace of briny ropes
A tug, a hauling-up

I tore out my hair and
wove with the strands

They broke into pieces then
I had a picture of her

She was all split ends
I stared at it for long hours

Wondering
If it was a true likeness

If she exists
If loyalty is a linear concept

strung from one body
to the next, or if

in the breakages there is a kind
of mercy, the way a fish

feels when the knife
slices away its breathlessness

Waste Thread

Buddha says we are all capable of waking up.
The human mind is nothing but sky-flowers.
Cataracts, clouds. Perhaps because I value the body
that made him, I cannot see my son clearly;
he dashes this way and that, wet petals, blur.

Penelope weaves thread all around her body and waits

Dish soap wringing my wrists.
Suds digging into the creases
of my palms. Needles, thimbles,
diapers. Shells on my dresser

arranged by color. Horizons
straight and empty
as a washing line. My son's
small, soft hand in mine.

Something I dreamed:
his toy ship capsized in the bath,
all hands lost. Smearing bubbles
on his face: *who am I?*

I wake with aching wrists.
I begin again. Sunrises with
him on my lap, reading stories
until we can see our shadows.

Something that happened:
Closed doors. Calm seas.
A year. The year my husband left
or my son learned to walk.

Dreams where I can fly.
Dreams where I don't live here.
Dreams where I am happy.
Dreams I push away.

Something I dreamed:
my body was tattooed all over
in white light. It faded
but when I flex my hands the ink

still stings. Soap bubble stretched
until the oily substance pops
and becomes a faint wet sprinkle.
Ways I ward against nightmare:

Crumbs on shale. Megalodon teeth
sewn in my pillow. Lavender sachets
in my hair. Nails pinning dress
to collarbone, slip to thigh.

Dreams where I grow fangs.
Dreams where I shed skin.
Dreams where I frighten him
or he doesn't know my name.

Something that happened:
A tattoo of my husband's name
in invisible ink on my shoulder.
Was that a dream? This wasn't:

my son catching fireflies in a jar.
Long dusks. Seamless days.
Nets of mussels bound in foam.
New oil, tart as fresh grass on the wrists.

Something I think happened
or will happen: my hips, softened
and spread like weeds. Hands
that tremble on the dandelions

before snapping off the velvety heads.
Moon a white knuckle, cirrus like
cataracts. Coil of red thread, clenched.
Tearing at the tapestry in my sleep.

Something I dreamed: my eyes on stalks,
pendulous, like branches hung with heavy
grapes. The mind's secret morphology,
etchings of venation, mutated glitter.

Something I dreamed:
A night sky made of sand.
Lizards like jewels
flickering through the thirst.

Waste Threads

Do you think the mind nails us in time?
I think it is itinerant, jumping epochs each breath.
Only the body suckers us to now.

Cataracts, clouds.

Escape: trapdoors, secret stairs, deus ex machina.
No one talks about the grim, tender truth of it,
how the body binds us. And even if it didn't, the soft animal
moan of a child turning over in sleep.

Pietà

Make a claim about a painting, the instructions
read. So together we stared at a computer screen,
at a scene by Perugino. The student asked,
Why is the man sick?, meaning the pale
pearl glow about his torso, arms
at obtuse angles. He was both important
and, she hypothesized, rich: the wine and olive
garments of the mourners meant money.
There. She pointed. *That's his mother.*
They looked about the same age,
smooth-skinned and slack, he in death
and she with the Renaissance countenance
I now know is no serene mask but a bleeding,
a woman drained until only the papery
husk remains. She, cased in blue, remains.

Yes, I said, surprised she saw the bond.
How no one else would hold a body
so clearly dead like a baby, cradled
to breasts, as if asking for milk
to sweeten and seep again. No wife
would have quite that angle.
Hmmm, she mused, *it looks like Jesus,*
but there's no blood. The harm
must have been internal.

In the painting she holds half
a body, holding out for whole,
the skin side tender as underfeathers.
Bent like a seed-heavy sunflower over his face,
she sings him lullabies or tells him she is proud.
It doesn't help to know he wakes up later.
Do you ever come back from a moment like that?
Or by the time he had risen, had she drunk herself

numb, eaten a box of brownies, sat in a bath
so scalding her skin turned purple-pink,
tried to watch the world's worst TV show
so she would forget her son slowly dying
while she waited? *There would be more blood*,

the student announced. It's flu; the plague.
A pietà evokes pity, and yet her firm,
fragile touch, her face softened by
an unbearable, unbroken gentleness,
seemed to summon something more like
compassion; all the viral ills of our world
by chance or grace befell this skinny white man
in a loincloth. At least according to Perugino,
who painted them in the Tuscan hills.
The scene would have been different in reality.
Darker, dustier. Less olive drapery, more
blood. But the numbness, still. *She should
give him chicken soup*, she said, *or maybe
he's dead.* We stared at the oils processed
through pixels, the odd representation
of a mother's grief. How undone she is,
how nice her clothes. Her hands on the creases
of his wrists, smoothing his eyebrows,
the way she used to when he cried, or maybe
it felt like her own body had finally succumbed
to itself, and without resistance she let
the leeches suckle her, began the slow bleed.

Pulse Ox

To saturate: to fill a sponge.
A viscous heaviness.

Only this is not a matter
of weight, though weighty —

stats at 70 start alarms,
increasingly shrill.

Those warning beeps,
the sound of thin,

the sound of blood not
nearly red enough.

I hear them in my sleep,
those tolls. What they cost

in nightmare is the price
to monitor a pulse,

to keep replete: oxygen
the stuffing for a vessel.

CO_2 creeps into
the crenellations, like soap

in the pockmarked surface
of a kitchen sponge.

Squeeze it dry. Each lung
a hefted thing,

a buoy all broken and filled—
saturated—with brine.

Unliftable, the kind you must kick
down the beach, rings of barnacles

breaking off beneath. Or we're fine
with 88, as long as you're

knuckling back into the nineties
half a minute later.

The monitor cries out, not pain
but electric impulse. It registers

the same. The sound of beeping
in my dreams, under my fingernails,

stuck in my hair when I wash it,
scrub the scalp. Beeping,

infernal beeping, falls out.
A hard, sonic hail.

I am infested—no,
saturated—with the sound.

Morphine

He needed sleep. But morphine isn't rest; it's straying,
a forgetful amble into dreams that vanish
and reappear, blotches, ink-blots, little graves

for memories. Would he remember me? I was banished
to the waking world, unable to spool out
golden thread, or drop crumbs, and famished

but unaware, he would wander, pool to black
pool, thinking a drip of stagnant water
mimicked the sound of Mama's voice. Cruel

bit of healing. But the opiates did their work, bought
us time. He didn't wake. Maybe he wouldn't,
we began to wonder. He'd wandered too far, got

lost, and though his lungs and heart began to heal, he couldn't
open his eyes. We made bets over his bed—
They're blue! They're brown! They're the color of wet wood

covered in bright-green moss! They're the color of lead,
leaking. The drug tangled in his veins, his brain,
and it was almost dread every time he stirred,

began to flex those tiny hands, mangled by IV lines.
I heard it in my dreams, the dispenser beeping
when it ran out, and I'd rant. We sang to him,

wanted to convince him not to sleep forever.
Songs of sunrise, oatmeal, rain; lays of healing;
ballads of creeping lichen, pebbles, skeins, waxwings.

Then, one day, he looked at me and saw.
Blue, I told my husband. Like a Hubble Deep Field
photo, full of gas and pinpricked light.

Waste Threads

Motherhood is full of ways of knowing
that I had no idea I knew. Capacities,
skills. I do them and realize they're done.

No rulebook. No praise. The lack
is a kind of grief.

*

Every day this massive effort, every night this unraveling.
Things change, it all goes to shit.

What Does Penelope Fear?

Red eyes falling from the sky
Roe, plummeting,
squashed on the windows and between the flagstones
I run for my son, the house all in a panic, people
    shrieking and praying and stealing things
but he is standing in the courtyard
Lurid wet beads squish into the soil, between his toes
He is picking up handfuls and stuffing them into his mouth
Horrified, I run to him
but he ignores me, shouting, Mama, I can see! I can see!

He was screaming
like a cicada screams

My husband was
kicking him with a boot
Gray eyes bloodshot

The man had the head
of a cicada and they were
tearing off his wings
in great papery fistfuls

The sound of legs
scraping against each
other filled the air

A headless beast stalks my husband
like wind in the corn

What if the cauterized neck is dreaming
me, asking me to stitch its likeness
to the night, a constellation
bright and gleaming
What if I don't deserve any stars

After death my elbows and knees
will be plucked and hung
in dark rooms like children's mobiles,
gently rotating

What if these precious daytimes
don't belong to me
but the beheaded nights
which erupt from my body
like wasps from the husk of a moth

I go out into the courtyard and gather handfuls
of wet rocks, their round hard bodies
click in my palms

If I close my eyes nothing happens
Then I put a handful of wet
pebbles in my cheek
and the visions come back

Waste Threads

I believe I am only really alive for a few moments
each day. I wake up and am dragged back under.
Do you know what that's like, to see the surface
up there and so rarely breach?

This sensation isn't related to motherhood.
I've always felt this way. If anything, motherhood
breaches me more often. It holds me closer
to the glistening surface of things.

Anticlea Teaches Swim Lessons

Wind in the door like an ogre's breath.
So I creak down to the kitchen
and up the stairs, to bring my grandson
milk and sing him women's songs,
which are full of heartbreak
but nary a snarling beast.
I check under the bed,
behind the billowing linens.
We are a family of sailors, I say.
We know that water closes its own wounds,
that what gushes out is its essence
and its mask. We do not believe
in monsters. I kiss his small forehead
and tell him he must learn to trust the sun,
the stars, the instruments of light
that make our oceans navigable.
He is afraid if he swims in the ocean he will disappear.
So in the mornings we practice, each firm stroke
a kind of fib that the body believes.

Nausicaä Visits the Tarot Reader

Name three men you'll love.
Name six. Name ten.

All of them have the same initials,
which you carved into a log at fifteen and burned.

Was it the counting that mattered, the listing
and circling of options, the implication of ruin?

You'll live in a palace with a prince. You'll live
in a beach-shack with a sailor's son. You'll live.

This card is development, potential, possibility.
Under each symbol a thousand grains of sand

rubbing against each other, their shell-grind
and smoothing. It makes a looking glass of sorts,

the way hard-packed sand seeps water and holds
the scattering of the sky. See how reversed,

he is nearly erased, a dark reflection
in a dry pool. She leans away, luminous.

You love and you circle a name. You love so you cross
out a name, cancel its syllables in your mind. You love.

Remove the object. Remove the veil.
One day you will throw away the skin

on which you inked his names. I hate to tell you
there's more to life, so instead, a fortune:

You will live by an ocean in the ribs
of a whale. You will marry the moon

and you will have six children, two dogs,
and a harp, and you will drive a chariot made

of baleen and dulse. Don't believe me? Girl-child,
watch. See already how the list of letters burns.

Penelope Dreams of an Old Woman

There was an old woman who ate snakes
or had hair of snakes
No, she was covered in a warm soft fur
and named her babies after the seasons
No, her babies were dead, all but one
who had turned into a seagull
and flown back into the salt

People feared her stench but
mushrooms grew in her footsteps
and they were good to eat

She stuffed my throat with yarn
I choked and swallowed
balls of color, fray clotting my stomach
Bulging, distended, my stretch marks
white and glistening again

For a moment I was happy but
now I have many legs and many eyes
My children swarm from the broken
sac in my abdomen

I pick up my threads and try to
sew them back inside

There was an old woman
crying into a fire

Her tears hissed like snakes
No, they were not snakes but cicadas

No, she was a boy
and he missed his bed

He cried cicada tears
little muffled screams

His tears were useless
to put out any fires

The next day's weaving was
a mess of red and orange thread

I thought it was ugly
and disturbing

One of my suitors said they
thought it was my best work

In the dream I become
the gangly boy
fingers long as talons, nails
black as winter twigs

I cling to ropes and blow
a birthday wish
send it smooth-stone skipping
over glazed-hard hills

Now I am circling overhead
looking down at his skull
Skin pink at the part line

He scratches and his skin
falls away and out
wriggles a gull

We rise on thermals, hot air
venting upward
or else he doesn't exist
or else I don't

In the Dusk Before Sleep

She rubs opals against her cheeks,
murmurs until moths drawn to the glow
alight on her jaw and softly open
and close their wings.

This is vengeful wholeness,
skin once again sacrament,
scar-crossed map. I try to ask
questions, but my mouth is full
of stones and the words come out
granite. She hears me, though;
she's listening. She eats pomegranate
one seed at a time, biting away
translucent flesh with nubby teeth.

I know what she wants to destroy:
the hard winter, the body's rind
hunkered close to its bones.

Somewhere a barn is burning, horses'
eyes like oiled eight balls, roof charred,
shuddering. Now it rains, a hissing rain
severs the spiderwebs—a tearing,
light, ineffectual patter.

She skips moonstone across the membrane
of water, watches it sink. Waits.
Skittering over the surface, mayflies
rise like clouds of ash in a hot wind.

The Old Woman Dreams of Penelope

I ache like the rocks ache
when the fire leaves them.

Old beams lashed, fragile rigging.
I tend to forget my name.

In my dreams the city
hardens to hot stone.

In her nights my city
is a mirage in the dreamlessness.

She furrows her brow,
tries to wake up.

She tries to brush me out like tangles.
I catch in the bone-teeth,

will not be unknotted.
Hilt of the comb, hilt of the knife:

mere instruments. Dreams
the motive, the method.

We double, we doubt.
She tends the fire, ruined hulk,

wet slag. I fall through,
land in my life. This? Here?

Not wet nurse, not wicked.
Cursed or caused.

I ache with the empty
at the end of the dream.

Scheria

We live in the attic.
We have bright eyes and
wet wings. We have bodies
given over to empire.

We say *look at the stars.*
The diamonds are spilling
on the floor. We say
the creature in the attic
is a wild animal.

It is easy to believe in
omens like trumpets.
Kings on sea monsters.
Upside-down queens
carrying goblets of raw gold.
They imagine the harbor
bearing a great jewel, waves
lapping at the facets.

We say emerald waters will
strike the shoals. Our ships
will calcify to stone. The ocean will burst
like a pustule and from the viscera
will crawl a falcon whose wings
are waterlogged and swift as ships.
He will harry our enemies
and perch in the attic.

We say we are not we.

They call us hysterical, slave-
superstitious. We shake our feathers.
We gnaw on foreign words

like pig bones. Why do we
try to save them? We say we
have already turned to stone.

Instead of a flagship, sea-glass,
bijou. Fish, swimming at its base,
will butt their heads against it.
On clear days, we will be able to see
the sailors trapped inside
its clear-green walls, mouths
agape like eels. Men, taken
with its beauty, will swim out to it
and kiss it for luck. Some women
will refuse to look at it. When will
it come? We pull out our teeth
in anticipation, lay them on window-
sills, bone offerings. Gum rock salt
until the fragile tissue bleeds.

Waste Threads

Penelope is a woman on the edge
of terrifying power. Each night's
revision alters the truth.
She can't get her bearings.

That's what motherhood is like. That's what
mothering a very sick child is like—day to day
reality changes. It all gets pulled out from under,
so fast.

*

Living with Q sick was a nightmare. Living without him
was a nightmare. Either way, I could never wake up.

The Point of the Waiting Room

after Carl Phillips

During the procedure, I touched no one.
My father-in-law paced the long hallway. Hard light,
ice from last week's storm, bounced off long windows.
My mother-in-law was reading. My son's body
was being given to him or taken back totally,
depending. Heart unclenching, lungs like a man-of-war
lifting with the tug of a deep-sea current.

The waiting room, with its basket of toys for siblings,
uplifting magazines on self and health, a carafe
of very bad coffee, strived so hard for normalcy
it achieved a kind of cruelty in imitation.
Impersonally so; that is, none of us in the room—
me turning my piece of stone over and over
against my palms; the silent older couple
drinking from paper cups; the uncles, I guessed,
talking loudly of trucks and horsepower
as if what lay beyond the doors would glance
off their brassy talk—were chosen.
The children on their respirators slowly learning
to suck down air, or being asked to and failing,
or fevering in thin sheets, or clutching bears
and picking at a pulse ox: they were not a lesson.

And yet I know the waiting, the asking, the uncles
as they stood in their work boots, hands tucked
in their dungarees talking cab size and bed loads,
could teach me something about loss.
About the great, cold, lumbering quiet that forms
like frost on windows *in the face of what finally
is only the world*. But there was also this:
my father-in-law found the surgery doors.

When the surgeon de-scrubbed through swinging
hinges he leaped forward and grabbed her arm.
Speed-walked back through the hard light
that cut and cut at the skin to tell us, to tell me,
my boy would live. His face flushed with the telling,
as a man in possession of a great treasure he is giving away.
My mother-in-law folded her book and put it down.
The news was not a reward or a rhetorical gesture.
I tucked my stone into my pocket, no longer
requiring the comfort, or perhaps I only believe
in magic when I really need it. But not in grief
alone are we face-to-face with the world.
Sometimes, though grief strips us with unrelenting violence,
my mother-in-law begins to rearrange her purse.
Hands me a mint. I remember how the grandparents smiled
and the uncles kept talking. How we gathered our things,
suddenly awkward and out of place, and left quickly,
no longer confined to that small room.
I don't know if anyone else got out.

Stitches

In the story I was telling you, a young boy
was scrubbing his feet with a bar of soap.
He yearned to stick to himself.
He needed a mother, to sew on his shadow
with a children's needle, thread the eye
with her tongue out. *Boy*, she said,
why are you crying? Tiny knots
make dark ripples against the wound,
he could have said, or how dumbly
the shadow flops, I need stitches
to reclaim my skin. Peter Pan knew
his shade writhed in sun's glare, knew
to suds it on would suture himself home.
Alas for the slipperiness. *I daresay
it will hurt a little.* We cannot live
without a shadow self, my father claimed
at one point, as if this were helpful,
as if I did not already have smudges
under my fingernails from digging
at the night-drapes, the bleak bulk
of the stars outside. I counted the hours
I was away from you each night, counted
the number of life flights each day.
The blades slicing open the sky.
Each slippery hour. My scar was long
and puffy-pink, a knife's quick work:
weeping half-moon contour. Pan's scars
were on his tippy-toes, quick ticks.
Your incision is in your neck, seven or eight
loops of string slender as geese in Vs.
High migrations. Wounds in the sky
after they depart, calling. Below, the artery
severed and neatly tied off, like a gift.
It gave you life, that knotted ending, me

a hook for a heart, a crooked sharp
fear of clocks. *As if he had been clipped
at every joint. He fell in a little heap.*
In the bath, we suds the bindings:
little black twigs plucked from pink skin.
How I mourn them. How we both flinch
in noon's bracing light.

Fever

He's hot as molten
silver, poured
off tips. Moon-
bright burn. He stirs.
He heats up. He flickers.

I wipe down his forehead
with cool cloth. Wipe down
the counter six times.
Bustle. Command.
Mash silver drops
in my palms and toss
them over flameless
sand with a gesture from
a wedding. An exorcism.

Dust storms,
dry lightning. Imagine
his spirit untethering
from its organs, tissue
still clinging
the way chicken
fat clings to the skin
when you quarter a bird.

Keep it together,
I tell my husband.

Imagine scraping
the spirit from his skin,
pouring annealed silver
scooped from his cheeks
into jars and storing them
in cupboards.

Imagine ice, vast
continents of it.

A cold. A fever
is nothing to fear,
the body's natural
defense—

but imagine a single
stroke, body
a pillar of soot.

See him standing
in the sand, black
statue in the shape
of a boy.
How it crumbles when
I reach for his cheek.

His little laugh,
shuddering up
out of its container.

Calm down,
I tell my husband.

But I am running through
the desert with a watering pail
sprinkling all the hungry
grasses with wet.

Changeling

We left behind our borrowed scrubs
and thank-you notes for the surgeons
and something else, something I
should know but can't remember,
some intimacy, some former idea
of the body as—no, it was not
the body, ever, but a different kind
of haven. We left it behind. Or it
never existed. Look, there's no point
in not asking: Did we escape,
or didn't we? I think about this
constantly. In the kitchen I push
on a loaf and it yields and yields
and the yeast are exhaling their
death-breaths into the flour.
I don't know how to make bread.
I don't know who lived and who
made it home. Instead,
I cook him plums. He's just started
to eat soft fruit. They told me to
strip the purple skin, flappy
on the flesh, but when I do
it recalls the viscera of sunrise,
yellow-pink pulp deliquescing
over the rooftops, the helicopter pad,
the peace garden, that useless
pile of weeds. One botanical use
of *deliquesce* is to form many small
branches. In which universe
are we living now? The one
where he lived, the one
where he died, the one
where I die, the one
where we all live

and eat plums together.
Whose child am I feeding?
Whose hands are disemboweling
plums? He flips the spoon
and dumps it, grins at me.
His lungs like dead moth's wings.
Heart clenching its beats
like a clam clutching
seawater. Leaky
fist. He laughs
as I cut away the soft parts,
the bruises, the narrow
tear-shaped seeds. He opens
his mouth like a boy, this creature
who came home with us.

Waste Thread

Summer skies as bland as a baby's conversation.
Baubles, babbles. So easy to get lost in the nothingness.
You go numb, all that blue.

*

Transform into a less pleasurable object:
pear, wine bottle. Bottom-heavy still life.
Apple with a slice cut out, just starting to brown.

Penelope Learns to Lucid Dream

I cried out like an insect cries out
when it is being impaled on a small
toothpick for a child's collection

Like the self I knew slithered out
and I was just the dry skin in the shape
of a woman, faceless and papery

Like chitin sleeks in the sun,
peeling away all the paper
and clawing at the guts underneath

My balcony used to be covered
in hyacinth now
it is mute stone I fear
the lack of flowers

I have let moss grow
on my body
as arm hair
as pubic hair
let it creep over
the skin and lock
its tendrils into the
soft space between
my thumb and my wrist

I noticed this morning moss
growing on the shade side
of the terrace
Tile floor littered with sap
and leaf-tear
Wrists stained with tree pollen

Fingers picked and picked
leaves from the weft
Pulled tender shoots from threads
They curled around the shuttle, clung
like a baby's grip
Tiny pea fronds, mint sprouts

I thought if I plucked them all out
I would wake up
Eventually I swam to shore and was rescued
by a giant dog who licked all the green
off my body

Underneath I was clear at the sky
and the sun shone through me
Like a tongue when
you rinse all the salt off it

I knew that
I knew The body
felt its rightness
A woman with
a fish tail No
a monster with
a woman's voice No
a riptide
in the hollow
of the throat
Its bone pull

Why when I sing
does it sound
like corpses
dancing Their joints
hinged so delicate
nested inside
each tender reunion
of finger and

wrist I sing
what I know
All the bones are
burnt All the memories
I knew were true
before I knew
what singing was

Waste Thread

When I see through my eyes and not my brain, I am
    really seeing.
When I walk with my feet and not my desire, I am
    really walking.

Lethe

When we kneel by the creek
chorused by damselflies, murky
in places with algae and moss, in others
tittering away over rocks, cup the cold
in our palms and sip, we are supposed
to forget everything. Let these boundaries
define you, they say; luxuriate in
the constant trickle and flowing away.
We trace fine wrinkles in our hands,
wonder how they got there. Some of us
have scars, some of them are deep
and only look healed over.
Those ones sit by the creek
and drink and drink and drink.

The forgetting courses in our blood.
So Achilles, no longer burdened
by that ridiculous shield,
takes up sewing. Picks delicately
at knots of embroidery, fastens
crocheted roses to his shirt hems.
So Ajax in his anger simmers
a good soup, goulash full of paprika
and pepper, and stirs the whole
concoction with his sword.
Nobody judges him. Charon
rests in his canoe with his eyes closed.
Beside him are one hundred dry flies,
carefully tipped with iridescent
flecks of abalone and mussel shells.
He hands them out to passengers
as a form of encouragement:
light breaking through the wings
of a hovering creature.

Despite the river's assurances,
we sometimes wave our bodies like props
in some half-remembered play.
Sometimes our hands crack like maps
of waterlessness. Sometimes Achilles
cries himself to sleep. We need
to keep drinking. So Anticlea starts
a fishing club. She wades in
to her knees until the calves
clench and casts her line
into the blue pool. One day,
she catches the biggest fish of her life,
sleek and muscular and handsome.
As she snicks the hook from its jaw
and lets the waters flush into its gills,
she vows that she'll never tell anyone,
not ever, what she's done.

Algal Bloom

Some kids across the reservoir are smoking weed
under a fir bough. They think it hides them.
The water is green as the old statue of Joan
in the park, a bright and aged copper,
and it ripples, trying to wriggle
out of itself, settle into some better shape.
The reservoir basin hums, every so often,
with the exclamations of stoned teenagers,
and I'm playing hooky, lying on my back
among the blackberry tearing through the ivy
and the soft mossy treble clefs of wild grasses.

It's hard to explain how I suddenly know this,
the way I know the taste of that fetid water
against my ribs, but I remember now that
I loved before I knew what it meant.
I tasted it briefly in the hills above Florence
where I used to walk in September heat
as flies buzzed in the straw-grass,
preening over some boy who wrote poetry,
as if that landscape, with its old stone walls
and trees as dark as coal nubs, were appropriate
for that kind of crush. Then, exhausted by the odors
of my own sifting, restless body, I would climb at dusk
above the city where monks lived and sit alone
in the stone-dark dust of the cathedral until
voices came like moths, white-winged
and hoary and beautiful, out of the grates
below the apse. Not heavenly but thick
with the dust of the crypt and the heavy
brass notes of medieval songs, chanted for
centuries by lonely men with crumbling books,
their voices in search of the darkness
beyond the obvious light.

For it's not obvious, how I came to love a child
I've never met. It hasn't been hidden, just unimportant,
like the plaque at the bottom of historical statues,
or how many legs the iron horse is lifting, as if
whether the person fell in battle or died of cholera
or was burned at the stake would matter
to some kids getting high a century later.
Still, despite my lack of attention,
the pleasure of listening drew me back.
It slid across my eyes at night,
a moon-coin paying my passage back come morning.
It was an old currency worn into faceless grooves
and wordless slogans, a comfort to rub again
and again in thoughtless moments.

No one ever taught me how to pray.
It doesn't matter, does it; I know the coppery
burst on the tongue, the sense of rest.
I know the moon can change and change
and look so familiar, that the sea labors
for each break, a birth that's never new.

But the algal bloom is still, thick but not stagnant,
a body finished with its spurts, letting the ease
of symbiosis creep over its exposed surface.
Waiting there long enough to be over *azure*
and *beauty* and *shimmering* and all that.
Waiting for the sound of darkness
like a scrape in an old keyhole, blotch
of sun on the concrete walls.

Waste Thread

She knows so much more than she knows.
She isn't a side-story. Soon she will wake up
and realize she dreamed it all. She fights it
because it will change her, but the dream
is fighting its way out of her. She's inhabited,
possessed, by a woman she can't help
wanting to be. It will destroy her life, but
she already feels monstrous; this is just
the outside and inside beginning to match.

Penelope Revises the Story

I tore out the weaving about birds
Prosaic, beneath my skill, besides

The birds are actually bats
and the young man with no name
blows sonar over the waves

It never bounces back but
last night it hit me
and pinged

He stretched skin-wings
mewled once
but the ship did not turn

so this morning I am working
on a design in three phases
A foreground of water
A background of water
And in the center
a small black dot

This morning I ran into the kitchen shouting
Give the men some wine or they will riot!

What men, my son asked me
coloring a page about dolphins

Hello Mama
Did you know dolphins have names?

I sat down next to my son
Tell me their names I said pointing

and in a voice like a bubble escaping underwater
he began to explain how dolphins communicate

How the land was a bed over which had once moved
a great body of water, a great rushing

The fossils of crayfish were cut into the rocks
I had run my fingers over their etchings

and knew I had caused their deaths, though
I wasn't sure how

I woke up desperate to please somebody
but there was no one there

I ran my fingers along the underside of the table
feeling for knife marks in the grain

Song to Call a Body from the Salt

Do you recognize the constellations yet?
The bear, the cored apple, the crab? The mother
with her hands full of stars,
juice slipping between her fingers,
her anklebones stiff with salt?
She's patient, but she's frightened
that you will not recognize her
small mooring, will slip past on ocean's
fickle current. That the brine
will drag you back. Have I, with my gift,
pulled down the instruments of navigation,
made the sky a featureless blank?
Can you see out there? Even the shore
does not know where it stops.
How can I expect you to steer
in the vast gray fogscape, how can I
expect you to hear me when I sing
journey-songs in a language you
don't speak, when language itself
is a lighthouse facing inland?

Notes

Quotes
All quotations from *The Odyssey* come from the Robert Fagles translation, published by Penguin Classics.

"Song to My Child in the Salt"
Amniotic fluid is about 2% salt. In contrast, oceans are about 3%.

"ECMO"
Extracorporeal Membrane Oxygenation (ECMO) is a heart and lung bypass machine. Often used in transplants and heart surgeries, it is now sometimes used as a last-ditch life support effort for very ill infants. One of the child's carotid arteries is cut and connected to the machine, which pumps oxygenated blood through the attached blood vessel, allowing the lungs to rest and heal. In those infants that survive, the severed carotid is tied off and their brains reroute blood flow to their brains through other arteries.

"Anticlea Teaches Swim Lessons"
Anticlea is Odysseus's mother, Telemachus's grandmother, and Penelope's mother-in-law. She is dead when she appears to the hero in the underworld, a shade questioning why he has come to this dark land. Her son had been gone many years before she died of grief, which is to say, she lived many years before that. In a house run by women, she likely had a lead role in raising her grandson.

Great fires flow between us, terrible waters,
the Ocean first of all—
—*The Odyssey*, Book 11

"Nausicaä Visits the Tarot Reader"
Nausicaä is a young girl on the cusp of womanhood. She
chances on the hero naked on the beach; there's some
innuendo; she acts with selflessness and a strong head on
her shoulders, but probably develops a bit of a crush.

Now who's that tall, handsome stranger Nausicaä has in tow?
Where'd she light on him? Her husband-to-be, just wait!
But who—some shipwrecked stray she's taken up with,
Some alien from abroad?
—*The Odyssey*, Book 6

"Penelope Dreams the Old Woman"
Nausicaä's servant, presumably an enslaved woman
captured in a raid, is mentioned briefly at the start of Book
7 of *The Odyssey*. If she was enslaved as a wet nurse, she
was likely nursing her own children before she was taken
to nurse the princess.

…Nausicaä made her way toward her bedroom.
There her chambermaid lit a fire for her—
Eurymedusa, the old woman who'd come from Apiraea
Years ago, when the rolling ships sailed her in
And the country picked her out as King Alcinous' prize…
—*The Odyssey*, Book 7

"Scheria"
As punishment for escorting the hero home, a Scherian
(Phoenician) ship is turned to stone in the harbor. Many
ships have come and gone through that harbor, bearing
women like Eurymedusa on slave convoys.

He'd say Poseidon was vexed at us because
We escorted all mankind and never came to grief.
He said that one day, a well-built ship of ours

Sailed home on the misty sea from such a convoy,
The god would crush it, yes,
And pile a huge mountain about our port.
—*The Odyssey*, Book 13

"Stitches"
Italics come from the novel *Peter Pan* by J.M. Barrie

"The Point of the Waiting Room" responds to Carl
Phillips's poem "The Point of the Lambs."

Acknowledgments

Many thanks to these journals for publishing the following poems:

The Healing Muse: "Chest Tube"

Intima: "Morphine"

Pangyrus: "Changeling"

Rogue Agent: "Penelope Pregnant"

Stirring: "Between"

Stone Poetry Quarterly: "Stitches" and "Algal Bloom"

Gratitude

Thank you to the many people who gave their guidance and support to this book: Rick Barot, Jenny Johnson, Greg Glazner, Kevin Goodan, David Biespiel, and the many wonderful faculty members at RWW whose workshops enriched my understanding of language, lyric, and story.

Thanks to all the Sonnet Cohort, for your close reading and companionship (Farelli's forever!) and especially Maureen Hunziker, my poetry wife.

Thank you to Bethany Reid for believing in this manuscript and choosing it as the winner of the 2025 Sally Albiso Award.

Thank you to my writing group, Stephanie Smith, Kaitlin Barker Davis, and Melissa Poulin, who bring joy and solidarity to both mothering and art-making.

Thank you to my parents for their consistency. Your love has been the foundation that made art feel possible. Deep gratitude to Brenan Dwyer for grouse sessions, pick-me-ups, mutual artistic admiration, and imaginary baseball.

Thank you to Hank, who watched the kids so I could write, and who was steadfast and kind through our hardest early days of parenthood. Thank you to Quinn, who transformed me utterly, and to Fiona, who healed the cracks. I love you both as big as the sky.

About the Author

Caitlin Dwyer writes, parents, and teaches in Portland, Oregon. She studied English at Pomona College, where she edited the literary magazine, backpacked the Sierra Nevada mountains, and signed up for far too many clubs.

After three years teaching and writing in China, Caitlin got her Master of Journalism degree from University of Hong Kong; her essays have since appeared in publications such as *Narratively*, *Longreads*, and *Creative Nonfiction*. She also creates podcasts and audio journalism.

Caitlin received her MFA in poetry at the Rainier Writing Workshop through Pacific Lutheran University. She teaches writing at Portland Community College, where she works primarily with first-year, first-generation college students. In her free time, she is either reading, wandering in the woods, or playing "the floor is lava" with her children.

www.ingramcontent.com/pod-product-compliance
Lightning Source LLC
Chambersburg PA
CBHW020754130626
46554CB00006B/2189